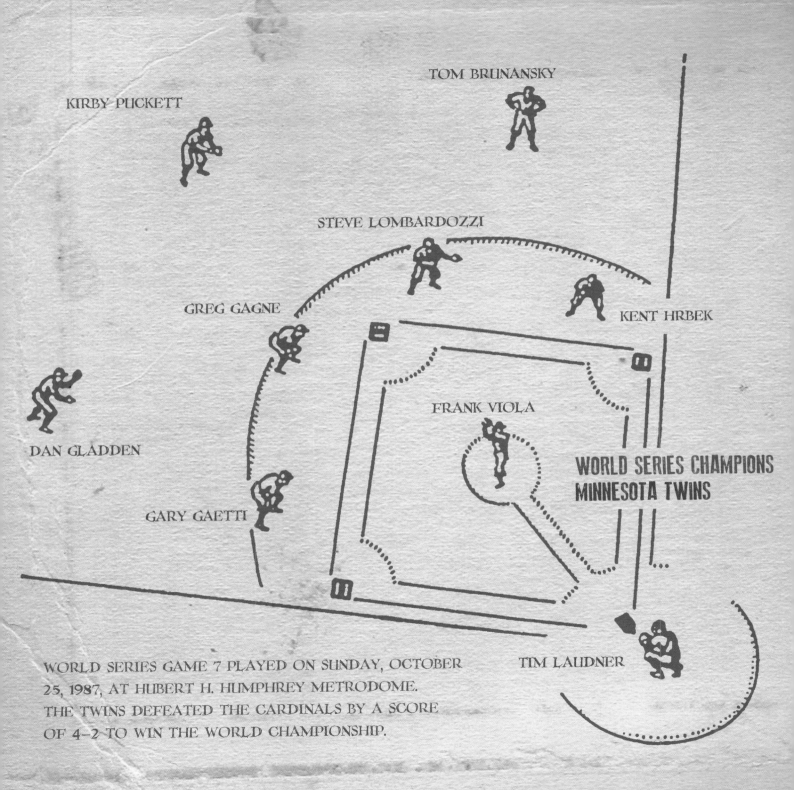

TOM BRUNANSKY

KIRBY PUCKETT

STEVE LOMBARDOZZI

GREG GAGNE

KENT HRBEK

DAN GLADDEN

FRANK VIOLA

WORLD SERIES CHAMPIONS
MINNESOTA TWINS

GARY GAETTI

TIM LAUDNER

WORLD SERIES GAME 7 PLAYED ON SUNDAY, OCTOBER
25, 1987, AT HUBERT H. HUMPHREY METRODOME.
THE TWINS DEFEATED THE CARDINALS BY A SCORE
OF 4–2 TO WIN THE WORLD CHAMPIONSHIP.

WORLD SERIES CHAMPIONS

MINNESOTA TWINS

SARA GILBERT

CREATIVE EDUCATION

Published by Creative Education
P.O. Box 227, Mankato, Minnesota 56002
Creative Education is an imprint of The Creative Company
www.thecreativecompany.us

Design and production by Blue Design (www.bluedes.com)
Art direction by Rita Marshall
Printed in the United States of America

Photographs by AP Images (Elise Amendola), Corbis (Bettmann,
Minnesota Historical Society, Brian Snyder/Reuters), Getty Images
(Chicago History Museum/Archive Photos, Diamond Images,
Stephen Dunn, Focus on Sport, Hannah Foslien, Judy Griesedieck/
Time & Life Pictures, Leon Halip, Bruce Kluckhohn, Richard
Mackson/Sports Illustrated, Jim McIsaac, Ronald C. Modra/
Sports Imagery, National Hall of Fame Library/MLB Photos, Tom
Pigeon/Allsport, Rich Pilling/MLB Photos, Bill Polo/MLB Photos,
Louis Requena/MLB Photos, Joe Robbins, Herb Scharfman/Sports
Imagery, SooHoo/MLB Photos, Tony Tomsic/MLB Photos, Tim
Umphrey, Alex Wong)

Library of Congress Cataloging-in-Publication Data
Gilbert, Sara.
Minnesota Twins / Sara Gilbert.
p. cm. — (World series champions)
Includes bibliographical references and index.
Summary: A simple introduction to the Minnesota Twins major
league baseball team, including its start in 1901 as the Washington
Senators, its World Series triumphs, and its stars throughout the
years.
ISBN 978-1-60818-267-1
1. Minnesota Twins (Baseball team)—History—Juvenile literature.
I. Title.
GV875.M55G55 2013
796.357'6409776579—dc23   2012004261

First edition
9 8 7 6 5 4 3 2 1

Cover: Catcher Joe Mauer
Page 2: Center fielder Ben Revere
Page 3: Pitcher Johan Santana
Right: Catcher Earl Battey

M

TOM KELLY

P

JACK MORRIS

RF

TONY OLIVA

OF

CHILI DAVIS

CF

KIRBY PUCKETT

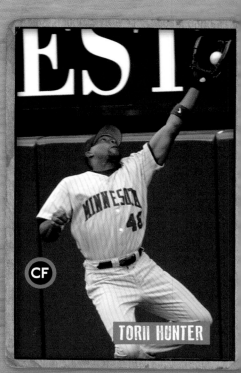

CF

TORII HUNTER

TABLE OF CONTENTS

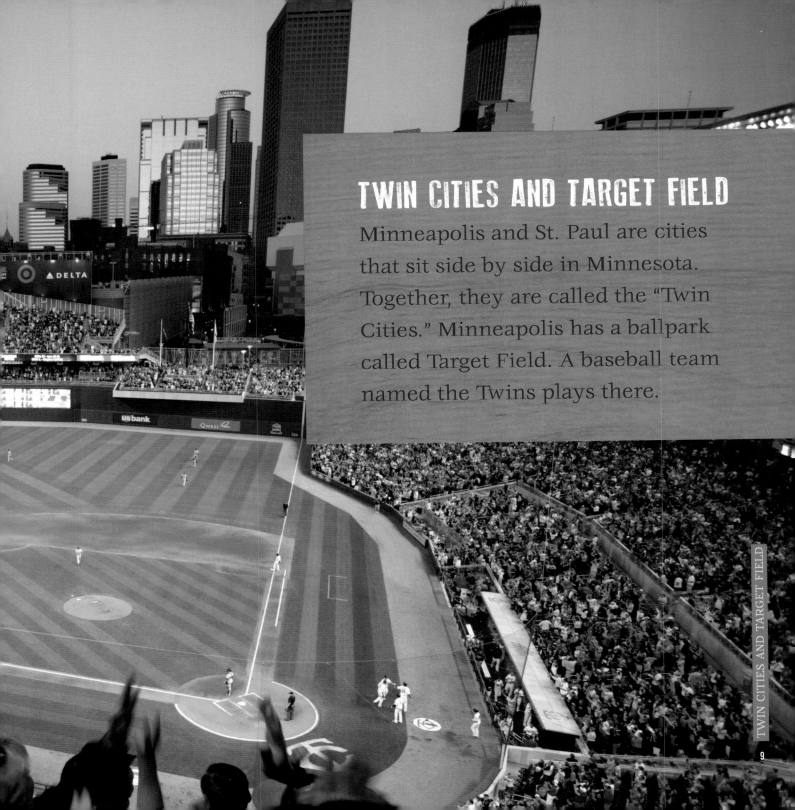

TWIN CITIES AND TARGET FIELD

Minneapolis and St. Paul are cities that sit side by side in Minnesota. Together, they are called the "Twin Cities." Minneapolis has a ballpark called Target Field. A baseball team named the Twins plays there.

RIVALS AND COLORS

The Twins are a major league baseball team. They play against other major-league teams to try to win the World Series and become world champions. The Twins wear red, blue, and white uniforms. Their main RIVALS are the Chicago White Sox.

SECOND BASEMAN ROD CAREW

PITCHER JIM KAAT

TWINS HISTORY

The Twins played their first season in 1901. They played in Washington, D.C., then and were called the Senators. The Senators played in the World Series three times. They won the championship once, in 1924.

1903 WASHINGTON SENATORS

P

BERT BLYLEVEN

2B

NICK PUNTO

P

FRANCISCO LIRIANO

P

BRAD RADKE

LF

DELMON YOUNG

SS

ZOILO VERSALLES

The Senators were not very good for many years. In 1961, the team moved to Minnesota and became the Twins. First baseman Harmon Killebrew slugged a lot of home runs to lead the Twins to the World Series in 1965. But the Los Angeles Dodgers beat them.

KIRBY PUCKETT

Center fielder Kirby Puckett helped the Twins win the World Series in 1987. But by 1990, they were in last place in the STANDINGS. They played much better in 1991. Fans were shocked when Minnesota won the World Series again that year!

Home runs by big first baseman Justin Morneau helped the Twins keep winning games. They got to the PLAYOFFS six times from 2002 to 2010. But they could not get back to the World Series.

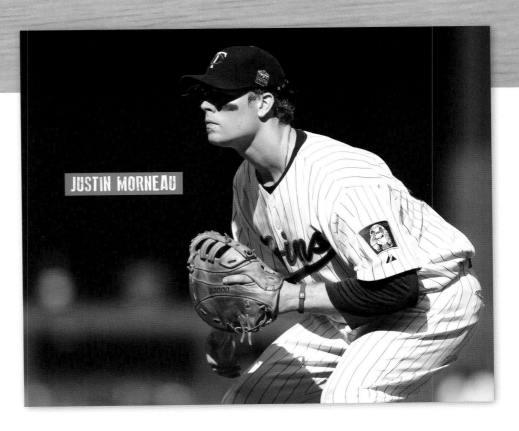

JUSTIN MORNEAU

WALTER JOHNSON

TWINS STARS

Pitcher Walter Johnson won 417 games for the Senators from 1907 to 1927. He struck out more than 3,500 batters. Bob Allison made great plays in the outfield for both the Senators and the Twins.

Tom Kelly became Minnesota's manager in 1987. He led the Twins to two world championships. Hard-hitting first baseman

Kent Hrbek played for Kelly. Hrbek made a lot of great fielding plays for the Twins.

Catcher Joe Mauer was **DRAFTED** by the Twins with the first pick in 2001. He became one of the best hitters in the league. The Twins hoped Mauer would help them win another world championship soon!

KENT HRBEK

JOE MAUER

PITCHER FRANCISCO LIRIANO

HOW THE TWINS GOT THEIR NAME

When the Washington Senators moved to Minnesota, the new owner wanted fans everywhere in Minnesota to love the team. He decided to name the team the Minnesota Twins, since it played in the "Twin Cities." It was the first baseball team named for a state instead of a city.

ABOUT THE TWINS

First season: 1901

League/division: American League, Central Division

World Series championships:

1924	4 games to 3 versus New York Giants
1987	4 games to 3 versus St. Louis Cardinals
1991	4 games to 3 versus Atlanta Braves

Twins Web site for kids:

http://mlb.mlb.com/mlb/kids/index.jsp?c_id=min

Club MLB:

http://web.clubmlb.com/index.html

GLOSSARY

DRAFTED — chosen by a team during a process called a draft

PLAYOFFS — all the games (including the World Series) after the regular season that are played to decide who the champion will be

RIVALS — teams that play extra hard against each other

STANDINGS — the rankings of sports teams from best to worst; they show how many wins and losses a team has

INDEX